Rage Bolus
& Other Poems

By Kerri Sparling

Copyright © 2021 Kerri Sparling
KerriSparling.com
All rights reserved
ISBN: 9798522862442

cover design by
Sasha Squibb
www.sashasquibbdesign.com

DEDICATION

This book is dedicated to my colleague, mentor, and friend, Paula Ford-Martin. *(SBCE forever.)*

(You can draw something here, if you'd like.)

Acknowledgments

Foreword by Korey Hood, PhD

Introduction

Part I: It Rhymes
    Rage Bolus
    an ode to my pancreas
    In My Head
    "Can you eat that?" – A Halloween Tale
    Murraybetes
    Won't you be my Valentine?
    Life, Undefined
    You Can Do This
    stop promising
    What Matters
    Is this diet?
    Bedtime Prayer

Part II: It Doesn't
    "But what if they get it?"
    Diabetes worrier
    click, clack
    catches air
    a window
    Privilege
    Haiku 3
    ghosted
    prepositional phase
    she still smiles

Part III: Homageish
    I carry my pancreas with me
    Beep, beep, beep!
    Silent Night
    Mr. Panc
    No Hitter Wonderland
    The Pizza Bolus
    Where the islet cells end
    Sorry, Poe
    Everybody Beeps
    There's room, I assume?
    Dexcom dance
    One Hundred Percent

rage bolus
/ rāj bōləs /

An aggressive correction dose of insulin administered most often after experiencing prolonged and frustrating high blood sugars. Often results in a hypoglycemic event. Does not always include math or reason.

>ex. *"I was high for hours and the carefully calculated corrections weren't bringing my blood sugar down, so I dialed in a big rage bolus."*

FOREWORD

The first time I spent quality time with Kerri was in a support group for parents with type 1 diabetes. As a psychologist, I co-facilitated the group and we tried to give tips and tricks about managing diabetes as a parent, and create a safe space to talk about worries. Kerri did not say a word. She was a new mother and she later told me if she had said anything, the flood gates would have opened and she would have cried for hours. Every time I saw her after that she looked away and said, "You're not going to make me cry!" As I read *Rage Bolus & Other Poems*, I realized why she asked me to write this foreword: revenge. She wanted to make me cry. And she succeeded!

When she asked me, I did ask – a book about diabetes poetry? Is this for real? You may be thinking the same thing, but I am glad you are here and reading. While I cannot write poetry, I can read it and appreciate the skills of a writer like Kerri. In her writing, Kerri captures the emotional side of diabetes, and that is close to me as a person with diabetes and when I work in diabetes clinics. Kerri so adeptly captures the surge of emotions diabetes generates, and frames it in the most unlikely way, through poetry. I hope that, as you read *Rage Bolus*, you too will be drawn to the content of each poem and its larger meaning. It is important for people with diabetes to share their experiences, be part of a community, and find ways to keep going when diabetes does not cooperate, which is often. I hope you will find that each poem struck a different tone, yet each one draws you in. Sometimes I laughed, sometimes I felt the same frustration the words exude, and sometimes I stopped and thought about the meaning of diabetes in my life. I think that is why this text is powerful – it perfectly captures what it is like to have diabetes and provides a new avenue to cope with diabetes. I was particularly drawn to "privilege," "what matters," and "in my head." (That's where she exacted her revenge!)

I also laughed out loud as I read through the anthology. I personally cope with diabetes with a mix of daily effort, humor, and support from others. So when I got to *beep, beep, beep!* and *everybody beeps*, I felt lighter. That is what I love about Kerri and her writing – she will draw you in with words, but it is the images and feelings the words paint that change you, for the better. I feel so honored to have contributed a very small amount to this anthology and am so thankful Kerri is a voice and presence in the diabetes community. Read on and let the poems be one more way to know others care about you and your diabetes.

Korey Hood, PhD
Person with diabetes (20+ years)
Psychologist and Professor, Stanford University

INTRODUCTION

My cat is big and fat.
Can you imagine that?
He likes to purr
And lick his fur.
I wonder why he does that?

I love words.

Always have.

The first poem I remember writing was about my cat. His name was Fluffy. (Evidence of being a little late in tapping my imagination.) It's not a poem that will echo through the ages, but it was fun to write, and fun to read out loud. I loved the way the words felt in my mouth, with their rhyming sounds matching at the edges.

The right combination of nouns and verbs, adjectives and prepositional phrases can make you laugh out loud. Or make you cry. They can be straight-up silly and goofy, making you have to hide your laughter in your sleeve. Or cause goosebumps to prickle up at the base of your wrist and travel all the way up to your collarbone.

Our words create stories, and the stories we share about life with diabetes have created connection points between people around the world. This community is **massive** and global; knowing we're not alone makes all the difference in the world.

Since starting a diabetes blog in 2005, I have had the chance to connect with the diabetes community, and this book is another way – a very different, slightly less narrative way – to share my lived diabetes experience. Reading the experiences of others has provided tremendous emotional support for me. It's honestly changed, and potentially saved, my life.

But this isn't a big book of serious stuff – there's a lot of levity baked into this writing. Some of the poems collected in this book might make you smile and others might make you chortle (or might at least make you want to look up the word *chortle – it's such a weird word*). You may see some of your own diabetes experience reflected in the rhymes. You'll definitely hear the influence of some of my favorite writers (they're honored throughout). I'm proud of each piece in this book, from the one about the pizza bolus to the one about insulin affordability, and everything in between.

I hope it makes you feel **something.** It's been the honor of a lifetime to have the opportunity to use my words to contribute to diabetes advocacy and community, and I'm forever in debt to you all for your support and encouragement.

(Quick note - I'm also very grateful for the few words that rhyme with "pancreas" and "diabetes." Man, some of those were a reach.)

Thanks for being here. And for reading.

Kerri Sparling
Diagnosed with diabetes in 1986

Part I:
It Rhymes

Rage Bolus

First, it's all the math
to calculate what's really needed;
the milligrams, the deciliter -
draft up the bolus, don't exceed it.

You wait and wait and wait
but then you see this high's a squatter,
and the bolus that you dialed in
seems the same as dosing water.

So then you take another crack
at reasonable dosing,
the calculations careful
and the math just so engrossing.

But hours pass AND YOU'RE STILL HIGH.
Is insulin on strict standby?
By then you realize there's no solace
from this high - so you RAGE BOLUS.

Rage bolus! Rage bolus!
You understand you might go low,
but frustration trumps your logic
so you dose with great gusto.

(But reader friends, I caution you
to bolus with great care.
A rage bolus can fix the high
But soft landings are quite rare.)

Rage bolus! Rage bolus!
It's when you're done with waiting.
You just go "argh!' and "what the heck,"
And plain give up on estimating.

Rage bolus! Rage bolus!
It's a phrase that you can yell
When you're high for no damn reason,
calm bids a fond farewell.

Rage bolus! Rage bolus!
That tendency to overdo
But sometimes you hit that breaking point
When logic just won't do.

Rage bolus! Rage bolus!
It's the end of all complacence.
You take whatever to correct a high
to battle your impatience.

Rage Bolus

an ode to my pancreas

Oh my panc is like big corn cob
That crapped out one September;
Oh my panc is like the laziest
Of my endocrine board members
So fair art thou, pain in the ass
So much work that you don't do;
Yet I will love thee still, oh panc
'Til you go get a clue.
'Til you go get a clue, my dear,
And the clue makes you un-forget;
Because you'll start making some insulin
From deep in your islets.
So fare thee well, my weaksauce panc
Oh fare thee well, you clown.
Because I still rise each day, my love,
Diabetes won't hold me down.

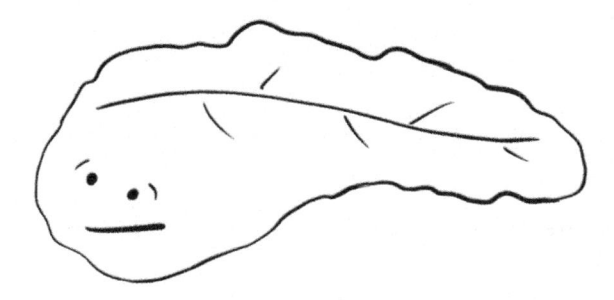

in my head

"Just don't eat sugar."
"Take your pills."
"Count your carbs."
"Avoid most thrills.
"Be prepared."
"Plan ahead."

But this disease
Is in my head.

I can't split up the thoughts around
My mental health and body sound.
Impossible to draw a line
Between "I'm sick" and feeling fine.

Just take my shot? And avoid stress?
Beware of cake? Test, don't guess?
The list of things disease requires
Aligns my needs to trump desires.

"I need juice."
"It might cause strife."
But sometimes juice can save my life.

It's hard to share
How much I see.
In every test:
Mortality.

Was seven then, when it arrived.
And since that day, I've stayed alive.
But not because
I've not had pie.
Or "just took shots."
I try.

And try.

The mental health
I have achieved,
I fight for – harder? –
Than A1C.

The demands put on a chronic life
Exceed "just take your shot."
We live beyond, we live out loud.
Mental health not an afterthought.

It's not a disease where you just "just."
It's more than simply "do."
But how I manage mental health
Will help me make it through.

"Can you eat that?" - A Halloween Tale

It's time to run around the neighborhoods!
Time to collect up sweet snacks and goods,
For tricks and treats and being merry,
... and some uninvited commentary.

"Um ... can you eat that?"
Yes, I can.
I can unwrap this Twix bar, man.
Can place it in my open mouth
Can chew it up and send it south.

These things? I CAN. My body can.
But choosing to is different, man.

Don't run your mouth
Or tell me what
You think I can or can't, tutt tutt.

I take good care
Of all my shit.
Especially with the shoddy bits.

So on this dress up fun time day
Please don't assume I've lost my way.
And that the haul of candy in my bag
Should raise up some big bright red flag.

I'm capable of collecting treats
And saving them for low BGs.
Don't lecture me about candy
As though it'll rise up and eat ME.

Trust that we know
And we find solace
In moderation
Or a well-timed bolus.

That life with diabetes does
Create an undercurrent buzz
Of worry, math, toil, and trouble
But we know how to burst that bubble.

We know how to trick or treat,
We know what we're ready to eat.
We know how to live with type 1.
We have diabetes, but we still have fun.

Murraybetes

Mornings start with graph checks and then we're off to live
Not all D things are solid, but we continue, we forgive.
Lots to tackle, lots to manage, lots to do in this narration
Though efforts might end up a little bit Lost in Translation

Details of the day go by in a flurry
But I'm blocking all the chaos like Rushmore Bill Murray.
One thing stays the same, one thing's on repeat
I'm always checking numbers to see how much I'm sweet.

It's a cycle that I'm stuck in, like it's always Groundhog Day
With the checking and the poking and the insulin melee.
"I've got you, babe," says my panc and it's right, it's our kinship.
So I stick to the D program, pseudo-panc right on my hip.

Tracking lows that feel like pranks, man.
All the juice that I just drank, man.
And the rebound after I tank, man?
I bust those highs like Peter Venkman.

Searching for the perfect mix of things that bounce my BGs
But that mix, it changes daily; that's the trick of diabetes.
Pre-diagnosis numbers? How I miss you.
But I'll keep working, searching like Steve Zissou.

It's a circle of the weirdest kind but no rest for the weary.
The repetitive cycle of this stuff can feel a little dreary.
But why bother? Why continue? Why give this constant f*ck?
Because we're worth it. Our lives matter.
And I'm guessing dead would suck.

Won't you be my Valentine?

Oh rotting, feeble pancreas of mine,
Won't you be my Valentine?
Won't you wake from your long sleep
And make some insulin, you creep?
What makes you sit, all shaped like a wiener,
Lazy and dull, with a pompous demeanor?
What makes it okay, that for your enjoyment
You've spent thirty plus years filing unemployment?
We need to start over; we need to be friends.
We need this whole type 1 diabetes to end.
I'm tired of shots and I'm sick of the lows,
So I think we should talk about ending this row.
I could use a break, my corn-cob-shaped friend.
I'd love to have 'old age' listed as my end.
I think that your time off has drawn to a close.
I'd like working islets, and plenty of those.
How 'bout it, old pal? Care to start working?
Care to start minding duties you've been shirking?
I promise to be an attentive best friend,
I'll thank you each morning and as the day ends.
I won't take for granted the hormone you make
And I'll forgive you for the last 30 years mistake.
I've brought you some flowers and a bookstore gift card,
In hopes that when I bring milkshakes to the yard
You'll be so inclined to jump start all those islets
Who've been holding their breath for so long that they're violet.

So what do you say, oh pancreas of mine?
Won't you be my Valentine?

life, undefined

"You have diabetes. You seem fine." "I am fine."
Diabetes makes me walk the precarious fine line
Between "I'm sick" and "I'm not" and the whole in-between
That makes diabetes invisible, and yet so **seen**.

"Needles? Every day? I could never,"
You could. And you would, and you'd do it forever
If that's what kept you from good life or harm,
You'd never think twice of needles in your arm.

"You seem fine." "I am fine, at least I think?"
I try not to let it push me to the brink
But all of my days are still "diabetic"
And on some days I feel frustrated, mad, or pathetic.

I can follow the rules and try to appease
The needs and requirements of relentless disease,
But even my best days are burnt at the edge
By the efforts that work their way in like a wedge.

"You seem fine." I am fine, except days when I'm not.
But I do what I'm told, and I learn what I'm taught.
And I'll keep working harder to keep from the claws
Of an illness that doesn't do "rewind" or "pause."

Will it stop me? It might, I can't lie – and that's scary
But between now and then, I throw all these hail marys.
It's life, **and it's mine**, and I won't let it bear
The weight of a heart and mind wrought with fear.

There are miles to run, and children to hold.
There are travels to have, and stories to be told.
Diabetes? Intense, and it looms, and it's giant
But I'm more than my pancreas. I've become self-reliant.

I host beta cells that checked out long ago,
But I refuse to accept the assumed status quo.
I'll work harder, think smarter. I'm not resigned
To accept limitations. **I live life** undefined.

you can do this

When you're dealing with something relentless each day,
It can feel like frustrations are seconds away.
There's the burnout, depression of chronic disease
The chaos that comes with attempts to appease.

We do blood sugar testing, precision carb counting,
We're wearing devices to aid in surmounting
The pressure of acting as pancreas stand-ins.
This whole diabetes can sure be demanding!

We lean on our doctors, we lean on our friends,
We lean on our families and try to no end
To master this monster known as diabetes.
We try, and we stumble, but get back on our ... feeties.

Because we can do this! I know that we can!
We can master this monster! We can draft up a plan!
Or just fumble days we're unsure how to weather.
The point is, we're in this, and in this together.

You can do this! You can. If I can, so can you.
(I'm the last diabetic who knows what to do.
I try hard to succeed in managing this whole mess.
I am so far from perfect, but I do my best.)

If you have diabetes, you are not alone.
You're part of a group that has blossomed and grown.
We're all living with this. We hold on to each other.
We'll get through today and move on to another.

You can do this. I swear. Even days that are rough
Come with moments that prove how you can be tough.
There's a life to be lived, one that I wouldn't miss.
So hold your head high. You can do THIS.

stop promising

She sits to eat -
all cavalier -
no strange food math
in 5 to 10 years.

She packs her pump -
now souvenir -
away forever
in 5 to 10 years.

She'll raise her voice
to volunteer
for something else
in 5 to 10 years.

She goes to sleep
and doesn't fear
what's coming

in 5 to 10 years.

What matters

I live every day with a pump at my hip
A meter close by, and a smile on my lips.
So many moments there are in my day
When it seems that my pancreas gets in the way,

Be it exercise, cooking or sleeping or driving,
I'm constantly checking to keep myself thriving.
And while my support team, my family and friends
Support me and hold me and love to no end,

I started to write because I felt alone -
The only diabetic as far as I'd ever known.
Needing to find others who understood
How a number could scare me, how a food could be good.

How I worried my eyes were damaged from cake.
I worried my worries were too little, too late.
How I worried my feelings were strange and unique
And that my diabetes made me some kind of freak.

I wrote my first post, took a great gasp of air,
Hit the big publish button and from out of thin air
My words were set loose to the great world wide web
And I wanted and hoped to hear what others said.

Within just a week, I had found several others.
Type 1 and type 2 and some fathers and mothers.
These people, they knew, and I felt less alone.
I feared less my future and all the unknowns.

The blogging took off and I chronicled things
Like my job and my friends and my engagement ring.
I poured out my feelings and dealt with my fears,
I let loose my laughter and reigned in my tears.

I felt so much stronger with all the support
Of the people who knew how my body fell short.

When I peel back the layers to what matters most,
It's not about how many readers I host.
It's not about stat counts and not about feeds.
It's not about fame and it's not about greed.
It's not about comments or big recognition,
It's about all the challenges of this condition.

This community knows me where I hurt the most.
It makes me feel normal, supported, and close.
I'm thankful for every day towards good health.
I'm thankful I'm not doing this by myself.

Endless thanks to the people who read these writers
And for making the burden we carry much lighter.

Is this diet?

I love going out on the town for the night
And having a meal by a soft candlelight
(Because I know, at a restaurant, meals are yummy;
For the food isn't prepped, touched, or cooked by me.)

But to dine with type 1 can be quite complex,
Because restaurant food has a whole set of specs
That require some SWAG'ing; carbs seem to inflate
As you wonder what's really down there on your plate.

"Excuse me, but does the salmon have a glaze?
Is it covered in sugary, caramelized haze?"
I ask of the waiter, tuning in as he states
That the glaze can be brought on the side of my plate.

My soda arrives, and I ask, *"Is this diet?"*
As I bring the glass up to my lips just to try it.
"It is," he responds, and he watches my face
As I try to assess the fizzy soda taste.

Moments later, I notice that something is wrong.
I'm not sure my thoughts are where they belong.
My brain is all foggy, my hands feel so weak,
I'm having some trouble with words while I speak.

Did I bolus too early? Did I miscount the carbs?
Is it something I did to make Dex go on guard?
There are glucose tabs right here in my purse,
But I know that I'll feel better if I have juice first.

My husband hops up, as quick as a blink
To go to the bar for something sweet to drink.
But it's not a big deal; I chomp tabs while I wait
For the waiter to come back and fill up our plates.

He comes back for our order, but I'm not quite ready.
My Dex shows my numbers as slightly unsteady,
With double-down arrows beaming; so unkind.
"Can I have an orange juice, if you don't mind?"

I see his confusion. The gears start to grind.
I hear the thoughts churning inside of his mind.
"She didn't want glaze, and her soda was diet.
The bread was right here, but she didn't try it.
What's up with this girl? Selective sweet tooth?
Whatever. My job is to bring her the juice."

He walks off to the bar to bring back something sweeter
While I quickly confirm the Dex trend with my meter.
"Here you go," and I down it in one giant gulp,
Not caring for class, or a straw, or the pulp.

"Thank you so very much," I reply to be kind
And try to regain some semblance of my mind.
My husband distracts me with soft, gentle chatter
While the orange juice fixes the thing that's the matter.

And the moments that pass are quick in real life
But it's hard for him, watching a low change his wife.
A few minutes later, things are as they were.
I'm no longer sounding all drunk, with a slur.

The waiter comes back with his menu pad out
And we tell him the entrees we'd like to try out.
Our date night moves forward without any trouble.
(The waiter's confused, but I don't burst his bubble.)

It's not a big deal; it was just a quick thing.
But it's always a riddle, what diabetes will bring.

Bedtime Prayer

Now I lay me down to sleep,
but we all know my pump will beep
So if I'm low before I wake
This apple juice is what I'll take.

Part II:
It Doesn't

"But what if they get it?"

"But what if they get it?"

The lady working at the JDRF walk table.
The person behind the counter at the pharmacy.
The pediatrician.
The mom who is concerned about her child's child.

But what if they get it?

And I answer through teeth I didn't realize I was gritting, a jaw I didn't realize was locked, a breath I didn't realize I was holding.

"We'll do our best."

And then she asks,
"But what if I get it?"

And I hold her close and tell her how happy I am,
and how proud I am to be her mother,
and how full and warm my life has been,
and I don't tell her about the worry because we'll worry later,
and say, "We'll do our best. We'll always do our best."

diabetes worrier

what's left in the butter compartment
(not actually butter)

Will my next shipment
of essential
insulin
arrive in its white
Styrofoam
box?

people complain
about the insane price
of toilet paper
and hand sanitizer

- that's the way
I've always felt
about insulin.

click, clack

click, clack
click, clack

my mother's wedding rings
against the bottle of NPH
she rolled between her hands,
mixing up the contents
then pulling the plunger
off an orange-capped syringe,
drawing up a dose
and plunging the needle
into the thigh of her seven year old

... trying to be gentle
but it's still a needle.

I think of this every single time
I roll a pen between my hands
and the plastic catches my rings
and makes that

click, clack
click, clack

sound of my mother
trying to
keep me alive

catches air

drinking without breathing,
I drain in seconds
eight ounces of sweet relief

thirst feels comical
and panicked
and consuming

because I hear through echoes
and see through fog
my hands small, twitching birds
threatening to

  fly
        off

if I don't drink until the straw catches air

a window

strange
to think
of my life
as a window
of opportunity
held open
by a vial
of insulin

privilege

Sometimes I think about

how my muscles would wither
and my skin would crack
and my kidneys would fail
and my blood vessels would collapse
and my nerves would succumb
and my heart would weaken
and my body would turn itself inside out in starvation
and how I'd be dead within days
without this tiny bottle.

It is not right
That people have to fight
For the privilege of dying more slowly.

haiku 3

Such a small bottle
with such a huge influence
on my whole damn life.

ghosted

I never blinked
or ever acknowledged you at all
just an organ
just some hormones
just my immune system going ouroboros
just
just
just didn't know how much
you mattered
until you ghosted me

Meals became math
and skin became home
to devices and needles.
Orange slices at soccer games were feast or famine,
depending on my mg/dL

and I didn't know how it infiltrated
until a classmate said
"Do you have enough for lunch?"
and she meant money
but I meant insulin.

or until I saw the word "blouse"
and assumed it was misspelled.
or until someone said
"when you're old"
and I assumed I'd be dead.

just an organ
just some hormones
just my immune system going ouroboros
just my childhood
just my children
just my life
just didn't know how much
your substance mattered
to the bottom line of me

prepositional phase

Childhood
Soccer games
First kiss
School dances
Going to the beach
Babysitting
First job
First love
Heartbreak
Progress
Adventures
Travel
Marriage
Love
Children
Pain
Rebuilding
Futures

A preposition dangling from each.
"... with diabetes."
One that doesn't minimize
Or empathize
Or sympathize

But synthesizes
a life
with complex parts
and elements
into a limitless and unfettered whole

she still smiles

It was six years, until me.

I didn't know her before my arrival, but from what I hear, she was just a kid who didn't see me coming. Running all over the place. Devouring every book she could find. This kid even read in the shower when she was that small. Bloated, damp books strewn about the bathroom. She tortured her sister relentlessly. She tried to play the games her older brother taught her.

She smiled a lot. And laughed out loud.

I'm not sure when I was called out to stay with her, but I've been told it was when she was sick as a little kid around her birthday. She had a fever that lasted for days. Lethargic little thing, under the careful watch of her ever-vigilant mother. I remember visiting her then, settling gently into her tiny body and making it my home. No one knew I was there. They wouldn't know for six more months.

Six months until me.

I didn't mean to embarrass her. But she started to wet the bed after I arrived. Six years old and wetting the bed again. She also had a ratty little pillow she needed to cuddle with when she fell asleep. I made her blood sugar so high in the middle of the night that she couldn't help it: she would wet the bed. And nothing, not the encouragement of her parents, the dreaded pee alarm, or the shame she felt, could make her stop.

So she quit that cuddle pillow cold turkey. "If I can't stop wetting the bed, then I'm going to stop this!" I felt bad. I had no intention of making her feel so frustrated.

She doesn't remember much of her own diagnosis, but I do. I remember when they found me. I remember when she peed in the cup at the doctor's office before she started second grade and they detected the ketones. They called her parents. Her mom and dad brought her in for follow up bloodwork. And then they found me. September 1986.

She didn't cry much. Her mom and dad brought her to the hospital, where she stayed for two weeks. Her parents bought her a stuffed Kitty that she toted around everywhere… the doctors became used to her little face and the presence of the stuffed animal. She said that Kitty was diabetic, too, and both Kerri and Kitty received injections. The fabric of the animal became a little stained from injecting saline, but it made her smile again. She didn't feel alone.

And she grew up. Even though I was there.

She competed in spelling bees. She tap danced for 15 years. She played soccer, albeit badly. (But I had nothing to do with that lack of athletic ability.) She kissed a boy. She drove her car. She battled with her parents and confided in her friends.

She wrote stories. She keeps a journal, still. She went to college. She moved out on her own. She succeeded. She failed. She adopted too many cats. She fell in love. She dreamed. And then she fell in love again.

She had six years, until me. People thought I would change her life, make her sad. Make her sick. Make her angry.

But instead, I've made her strong. I've made her fearless. And I've made her appreciate everything she has, everything she fights for. She hasn't let me make her choices. She refuses to let me own her. She controls me. When she is in her last moments, whether sixty years from now or today, she will know, with certainty, that she has Lived.

Really lived.

She still smiles a lot. And laughs out loud.

Part III:
Homage-ish

I carry my pancreas with me

(poem inspired by: I carry your heart with me by e.e. cummings)

I carry my pancreas with me
(I carry it on my hip)
I am never without it
(anywhere I go it goes, my dear; and whatever is done
by only me is your doing, my darling)
I fear no fate
(okay, that's not true)
I want no world
(for real, except
I'd love a functioning organ)
and it's you are whatever a meter
has always meant and whatever
a CGM says will always beep for you

here is the deepest secret nobody knows
(here is the thing that I lie about
and pretend not to think about
and try not to care about
but I really hope and I care)
and this is the hope
for a cure that will fix the pancreas inside of me

i carry my pancreas
(i carry it on my hip)

i carry my hope
(i carry it in my heart)

Beep, beep, beep!
(a diabetes-themed parody of: Little Blue Truck by Alice Schertle)

Alarm went "Beep!"
Dexcom purred.
Islet cells
remain unstirred.

Little Black Pump
came down the road.
"BEEP!" said Pump
to the big carb load.

Carbs said, "Yup!"
and winked an eye
When Little Black Pump
went bolusing by.

Food said, "Baaa!"
Exercise said, "Bump!"
"Yoink!" said stress hormones.
"Beep!" said Pump.

"Argh!" said the Kerri
(but her kids were asleep)
"Logbook," said her phone app.
Pump said, "Beep!"

"Nay!" said a cupcake.
Work said, "Jump!"
"Beep!" said the friendly
Little Black Pump.

"HONK!" yelled the dumb Panc.
"Coming through!
I've got tasks
But no follow through!

I haven't got time
to pass the day,
making insulin
along the way!"

ROOOM! went the Panc
Around a curve.
He saw high BGs
and he tried to swerve —

Into the high
Rolled the big fat Panc.
"What do I do?"
The pancreas drew a blank.

His heavy duty
islet cells
were on hiatus
for an undisclosed spell.

"HONK!" cried the Panc,
and he sounded scared,
but nobody heard
(or nobody cared).

Then ... into the high
BUMP, BUMP, BUMP,
was our helpful little hero,
the Little Black Pump.

Little Black bolused
with all his might
to help bring down
the blood sugar fright.

"Help! Help! Help!"
Pump cried from the sludge.
"Beep! Beep! Beep!
This high won't budge!"

Everybody heard that
"Beep! Beep! Beep!"
The DOC came running
(even those who were asleep).

Up at a gallop
came the blogosphere.
Twitter came, too,
And Instagram was here.

The web came in
with support and advice
and everybody helped
make that high play nice.

Head to head
and no one goalless,
they all told Pump
"Time to **rage bolus**."

The Rage Bolus budged
that heavy carb load.
Sending that high
back down in-range road.

All together —
one ... two ... three!
One last bolus
and the Panc was free.

"Thanks, little brother,"
said the Panc to Pump.
"You helped me,
Even though I'm a grump.

Now I see
a lot depends
on a helping hand
from a lot of good friends."

"Beep!" said Pump.
"Well this was fun.
Back to work, now,
Everyone!"

Yoink! Blargh! Nay!
Yup! Baaa! Sleep!
Diabetes soundtrack?
Beep! Beep! Beep!

Silent Night

(inspired by Silent Night, composed by Franz Xaver Gruber with lyrics by Joseph Mohr)

Silent night, well not quite.
Sleeping well? Not tonight.
Round yon Dexcom, mother and child.
Holy crap this graph line is wild.
Sleep when things settle down?
Sleep when things settle down.
Silent nap, holy crap!
Glucose tabs for a snack.
Dial down basal rates for a few hours
Knowing that others have nights just like ours.
When will sleep be a thing?
When will sleep be a thing?
Silent night. Finally, right?
Steady graphs, a delight.
Tucked back in, the kid is asleep.
All those devices won't make a peep.
The bedside table's a mess,
One day we'll all worry less.

Mr. Panc
(a diabetes-themed parody of: You're a Mean One, Mr. Grinch by Theodor "Dr. Seuss" Geisel)

You're a mean one, Mr. Panc.
You really are a heel!
You've made me a pincushion,
all those needles I can feel, Mr. Panc.
You make me require boluses before every meal!

You're so lazy, Mr. Panc.
Your islets are such shit!
Your shape is all corn cobby
and your betas all went quit, Mr. Panc,
You make me so frustrated sometimes I could spit!

You're just in there, Mr. Panc
You're a lumpy lump of cells.
You take all my tender sweetness
and my body just rebels, Mr. Panc.
Given a choice I'd give you back but I'm stuck with you and the band aid smells!

You've gone rotten, Mr. Panc
Thirty-one years ago you tanked
Your refusal to make insulin
is a cumbersome little prank, Mr. Panc
You're a rage bolus inducing little toadstool I won't thank!

You nauseate me, Mr. Panc.
Because my ketones sometimes run small.
You make blood sugars chaotic
even when I'm on the ball, Mr. Panc.
You're an appalling dump heap overflowing with the most
disgraceful assortment of dead cells
but hey thanks for still making enzymes at all!

You're a foul one, Mr. Panc
You're a nasty bag of gas,
Your uselessness makes challenges
that are a perseverance masterclass, Mr. Panc.

The three words that best describe me are as follows, and I quote:
"Still kicking ass!"

Walking in No-Hitter Wonderland

(inspired by Walking in a Winter Wonderland, by Felix Bernard and lyricist Richard Bernhard Smith)

Dexcom rings
Are you listening?
On the graph
Lows are blistering.
A beautiful sight
Is an overnight
Walking in no-hitter wonderland

Gone away
Are my betas
Here to stay
Is the data.
My Dexcom alarms
Protect me from harm.
Searching for no-hitter wonderland.

In the meadow we can build an organ
And pretend that he's a pancreas.
He'll say I'm so useful
We'll say no man
But I will do your job
You pain in the ass.

Later on
We'll check BGs
As we dream of a cure, please.
To face unafraid
The plans that we've made
Waiting for no-hitter wonderland
Dexcom rings
And I'm tuned in
On my graph
I'm improving.
A beautiful sight
I'm happy tonight
Watching my no-hitter wonderland.

The Pizza Bolus

(a diabetes parody of "A Visit from St. Nicholas" by Clement Clarke Moore)

T'was the night before Christmas and all tinsel's in,
Not a creature was stirring or making insulin.
The stockings were hung by the chimney with care
In hopes that my islet cells soon would be there.

My children were nestled all snug in their beds;
While visions of pizza boxes filled me with dread.
I took out my pen, assessed the amount
And settled my brain to complete the carb count.

When out on the lawn there arose such a clatter
I sprang from my chair to see what was the matter.
Away to the window I went with a fright
(And on the chair arm almost ripped out my pump site).

The moon on the breast of the new-fallen snow
Highlighted the ... thing? there at rest down below.
When what to my wondering eyes did appear
But a miniature Panc, looking all cavalier.

He looked like a corn cob, or maybe a penis.
I knew that he saw me, despite distance between us.
More rapid than eagles my insults they came,
As I whistled and shouted and called out his name.

"You stupid old pancreas! Where have you been?
It's been 30 dumb years since I've seen you again.
From my childhood years to now raising my own,
Diabetes is the only life that I've known!

And now you waltz back, sitting there on my lawn
Expecting me to give hugs or to kiss or to fawn ..."
But while I was ranting, the Panc, he just flew
Straight to the shed roof while I shouted, "Go screw!"

He stood there, so regal, and then, the rogue mutt,
He pulled down his pants and he showed me his butt.
And it became clear, as I fumed and I seethed,
That he came here to fight me, is what I believed.

So I steeled myself there, as the doorknob did rattle
And my pancreas came in my house to do battle.
He took out his betas, I whipped out a spoon
We stalked one another in my living room.

His eyes, how they narrowed, his islets, how lazy!
(I was glad Chris was out 'cause I'm sure this looked crazy.)
His droll little mouth was all knitted with rage
As he jabbed with his right, then down dropped the steel cage.

It was just me and him, in a fight to the pain
"If you won't make insulin, I'll go full hurricane!"
We fought there for hours, just me and that thing,
I had a black eye and he pulled his hamstring.

Until finally – finally – I landed the punch
That sent the panc reeling and hurt a whole bunch.
While nursing his knee and cradling his arm,
My pancreas said, in efforts to disarm,
"You've bested me for decades, and I owe you a prize.
So grab that there pen and now open your eyes.
There's a carb calculation, a quest for the ages,
And in minutes you'll know it, so mark up those pages.
You've won, fair and square, and I owe you some solace.
So Kerri, here it is: the **coveted Pizza Bolus**."

He spat out some numbers and fine ratios
And I scrambled to write down his mathematical prose.
By the time he was done, our fight fences were mended.
I would remain the Lead Panc while his ass just pretended.
And he reached out his hand to shake, sealing the deal
I extended mine back, not knowing how to feel.
But I heard him exclaim, as he limped out of sight,
"You've won this round, Kerri. Enjoy pizza tonight!!"

Where the islet cells end

(inspired by "Where the Sidewalk Ends" by Shel Silverstein)

There is a place where the islet cells end
And that's where diabetes begins.
In this place, you can stumble and things can get scary
Those moments when numbers make you feel so wary
And the burden is almost too heavy to carry
This is where **our community** comes in.

Let us leave this place where misconceptions grow
And the damaging articles win.
Where the blood sugar pendulum swings to and fro
And the mindset of fear leads to ... well, I don't know
Past the place where you're told that you reap what you sow
To that place we find strength deep within.

We'll all write with a purpose that's true and we'll know
That our words make a difference; the world we will show
What it means – "diabetes" -, and together, bestow
Our support on each other. **Our friends.**

Sorry, Poe

(inspired by "The Raven" by Edgar Allen Poe)

Once upon this Christmas season, as I pondered, within reason
Through my numbers, stolen from the memory
my One Touch Ultra stored.
While I noticed, nearly sleeping, all the records I was keeping
Showed a low that I saw, peeping, "Study me!" It did implore.
"I know you," I muttered, "Tricky low from nights before."
Lessons learned in spades, once more.
And the pages of my logbook, underneath my hand they shook
As I saw the low that plagued me on my nightly workout tour.
So that now, to still the beating of my heart, I stood repeating,
"Never workout without eating, eat a snack, I do implore.
Workouts make you low and then you must eat more.
Eat until you've been restored."

Ah, distinctly I remember, it was just this bleak December.
And I had just returned from work, surviving traffic jam galore.
Went to the gym and worked out hard, ridding my body of its lard
Counted all my workout carbs, those carbs are what I bolused for.
For those tasty, complex carbs
whom the pump was cranked up more.
'Twas only these and nothing more.

And I left my mind at home and worked out at the gym alone,
With nothing but some juice, my phone, and I forgot to test before.
So as I worked out hard, and sweating,
all the time I was forgetting
Never letting myself test and find out my blood reading score.
But legs buckled and I stopped, staring at the Gold's Gym floor.
"I'd better test or I'm done for."
Meter out and finger pricked, I waited for the finger stick
To ferret out my sure to be low hemoglobin score.
After seconds, I rang in with sweaty palms — 47!
And chugged the juice like I have never chugged the juice before.

I had to drink it fast or else I would have hit the floor.
A fall like that makes heads quite sore.

My face, once pale, restored its blush.
I gathered my things in a rush
And staggered to the car with levels rising more and more.
Keys in ignition, I remembered, that the bolus I had tendered
Covered more carbs than I rendered, rendered to my mouth before
I walked through those big glass gym doors.
Over-bolused, nothing more.

The lesson learned, I fear to lecture,
from this Raven-esque conjecture
Is that "just a snack" is not enough glucose for my body to store.
I've realized, through this event,
that working out is Glucose Spent
Just some tweaking saves my head
from crashing up against the floor.
I crank my basal down to even up the score.
In hopes of being low no more.

Everybody Beeps

(a diabetes parody of the song Everybody Hurts, by R.E.M.)

When your day is long
And the night, the night is yours for sleep.
When you tuck yourself in bed
For some rest ... well hang on
Don't close your tired eyes
Cause you wear a device
And everybody beeps ... sometimes.
Sometimes reservoirs are low
And need to be refilled.
So you get up out of bed (set off, prime on)
Remove the older site (prime on)
You fill with what you need
For three days ... well hang on
Everybody beeps
Takes comfort in the tech
Everybody beeps
Don't throw your pump, oh no
Don't throw your CGM
You feel like you're alone?
No, no, no ... you're not alone.
If your islets are a mess
And you're doing the best you can
When you think you've had too much
Of the beeps, well hang on
Well everybody beeps, sometimes.
But you are not alone.
Community is here.
All the time.
We're here all the time.
All the time.
So hold on, hold on
Hold on, hold on, hold on, hold on, hold on, hold on
Everybody beeps

There's Room, I Assume?

(a diabetes-themed parody of: Room on the Broom by Julia Donaldson)

The Girl has a panc
And islets that were blank
And a long history
With no pancreas thanks.

Oh but how the Girl worked
And how the Girl toiled
To keep diabetes
From making life spoiled.

But how disease wails
And how disease barks
As it moves to our bodies
And works to leave marks.

"Down!" cried the Girl
As she looked at her Dex
Wondering why her blood sugar
Management was complex.

It should be "count carbs"
And then calculate doses.
(A pre-meal lunch bolus
Should not cause psychosis.)

Dex looked at her sadly
And let out a BEEP
(As the Girl pulled her pump out
From hip, hidden deep),

"I am your Dex, as keen as can be.
There is room, I assume,
For a Dex like me?"

"Yes!" cried the Girl,
and the Dex gave a laugh.
The Girl tapped the button
And WHOOSH! There's the graph!

Throughout the day,
The Girl wrote and she worked.
Her daughter drew pictures,
Both cats went berserk.

The Girl laughed out loud,
All the memories brewing.
Memories of not knowing
What blood sugar was doing.

"Up!" cried the Girl,
when she saw, on her run,
That her blood sugar tumbled
Down to 81.
Then out from her SpiBelt
With a flourish of dust
She grabbed glucose tabs
And ate three in a rush.

"Why make the effort?"
Some innocents asked.
"Is exercise worth
Getting kicked in the ass?"

Then she said,
As the Dexcom went BEEP with intent
To let her know
just how low blood sugar went,
"I used to fly blind,
but now I have Dex
That helps me keep
blood sugar numbers in check."

Then, all of a sudden,
In the silence of night
Blared the BEEP from the Dexcom
That woke her upright.
It woke up the Girl
And it woke up her Chris
(And it scared both the cats
As they let out a hiss),

"I am your Dex, as loud as can be,
Get up soon, while I boom,
And eat tabs or candy."

"Grumph," said the Girl
As she stumbled from bed
And consumed the contents
of the fridge instead.

But thankful that beeps and alarms
Work to rumble
from deep, sleeping slumber
While blood sugars tumble.

"But it's a device!
It makes you mechanic!"

"I'd rather devices
than blood sugar panic."

Dex looked at her proudly
And let out a BEEP
(As the Girl checked the patterns
Before going to sleep),

"I am your Dex. I work hard as can be.
There is room, I assume,
For a Dex like me?"
"Yes!" cried the Girl,
on her Safety's behalf.
The Girl tapped the button
And WHOOSH! There's the graph!

Diabetes Dance
(a diabetes-themed parody of: Barnyard Dance by Sandra Boynton)

Stomp your feet!
Dexcom glance!
Everybody ready
For the Diabetes Dance!

Bow to the pancreas
Furrow your brow
Twirl with the pump if you know how.

Bounce with the blood sugars.
"Fiabetes, duck!!"
Dial in a rage bolus,
Such crap luck!

With a BEEP and a BOOP
And the lancet stabs.
Everybody promenades
Glucose tabs!

Prance with infusion sets
Cure all the mice,
Swing around pump tubing
once or twice

Stand with the advocates
Side with what's right
Raise your voice powerfully.
Use your might.

With a BEEP and a BOOP
Count your carbs not crabs
Another little promenade
Glucose tabs!

Check with the CGMs
Careful not to swear
Take another spin with the pump you wear.
Turn with tide of your constant data,
All take a bow, and high five to dead betas.

With a BEEP and a BOOP and
a low carb snack,
The dance today is done
but we'll be back

a human's resilient, 100%

(a diabetes-themed parody of: Horton Hatches the Egg by Theodor "Dr. Seuss" Geisel)

Sighed Panky, a lazy panc deep in the gut
"I'm tired and I'm bored
And I'm stuck in a rut
From making, just making insulin every day.
It's work! How I hate it!
I'd much rather play!
I'd take a vacation, or a long nap
If I could find someone to do all this crap!

If I could find someone, I'd kick back and chill …"

Then Panky thought, "Could Kerri be up for the thrill?"

"Hello!" called the lazy panc, smiling her best,
"You've nothing to do. Does this sound too strange …
Would you like do the work I do for a change?"

Kerri laughed.
"Why of all silly things?
I haven't islets or enzymes or things.
ME do your job? Why that doesn't make sense!
Your job is make insulin! The thought makes me tense."

"Tut, tut," answered Panky. "I know you're not me
But I know you can do this. Won't you hear my plea?
Just pick up that needle and draw up the dose.
Once insulin's flowing you won't feel morose."

"I can't," said the Kerri.
"PL-E-ASE!!" begged her panc.
"It won't be too hard, kid. Sorry to pull rank.
But I'm leaving regardless if you raise your voice."

"You're a jerkface," said Kerri. "Not to give me a choice.

I'm unsure how to do this. Details are the devils!
How do I keep steady my blood sugar levels?
What do I do? Can you leave me instructed?"

"You'll figure it out," and the panc self-destructed.

"The first thing to do," murmured Kerri,
"Let's see.
The first thing to do is to prop up this Me
And to make ME much stronger. This has to be done
Because diabetes can weigh an emotional ton."

So carefully,
Hopefully,
She searched, unimpeded
For the resources, tools, and support that she needed.

"I know that there's life found after diagnosis.
It's good and it's worth it. That's the prognosis.
I meant what I said
And I said what I meant …
A human's resilient,
One hundred percent!"

Then Kerri, with peers and insulin by her side,
Well she tried
and she tried
and she tried
and she tried.

She kept at it for decades
Despite feeling perplexed.
It requires work one day,
Again on the next.

It sucks! Then it doesn't!
But Kerri remained sure,
"My life's worth this effort,
(Though I'd still love a cure.)
I wish Panky'd come back
'Cause some days I'm so burnt.
I hope that my body thrives on the things that I've learnt."

But Panky, by this time, was far beyond near,
And was dormant for good now. Diabetes was here
And was staying, so Kerri, for better or worse,
Had a pump on her hip, glucose tabs in her purse.

Diabetes is constant, day after day.
But the life in its wake is still good, plenty yay.
And even on days when the Stuff is Way Blah,
Life with disease is not life without Awe.
"It's not always easy. Diabetes might test me.
"But I'll stay on task and I won't let it best me.
I meant what I said
And I said what I meant …
A human's resilient
One hundred percent!"

Some days it is simple. Some months are real hard.
Diabetes is something you can't disregard.
But a panc on vacation doesn't mean that you're broken.
"You can still do this."

Truer words never spoken.

ACKNOWLEDGMENTS

An enormous thank you to the Diabetes Online Community for being part of this journey as I found my voice. To my oldest DOC friends: Scott Johnson, Amy Tenderich, Violet, Tek, Nicole Purcell, George Simmons, Sandra Miller, Julia Zegarra, Shannon Lewis, Cherise Shockley, Manny Hernandez, and Dee Herman. To the dLife Editorial Team. To the Saucy threaders - Dana, Renza, Grumps, and Melissa. To my CWD and TCOYD friends and family. To Sean, Chris, Korey, and Scott.

To my mom and dad, who were determined to make sure diabetes did not define me.

All my love to Team Sparling. Seriously. All of it.

To all the words that sort of rhyme with "pancreas" and "diabetes" – thank you for making yourselves known.

To you, for reading this.

♡

And to my pancreas – you stink.

ABOUT THE AUTHOR

Kerri Sparling is a writer, poet, and speaker who has dedicated her life to amplifying the patient narrative. Since 2005, she has been a leading voice in the patient advocacy space, sharing her personal story of over 34 years with type 1 diabetes while helping share stories from others in the patient community. Kerri has worked to bolster the influence of patient stories in the healthcare space, from academic journals to keynote presentations around the world.

She is best known for her work as a patient storyteller at SixUntilMe.com, and is the author of *Balancing Diabetes* (2014) and *Rage Bolus* (2021). You can keep up with Kerri's latest work at KerriSparling.com

Kerri lives in Rhode Island with her husband, their two kids, and a bunch of fancy notebooks she's afraid to write in because she doesn't want to waste them.

To connect with Kerri, you can email her at kerri (at) kerrisparling (dot) com.

Made in the USA
Las Vegas, NV
07 August 2024